NorthWord
PRESS, INC.

Minocqua, Wisconsin

PHOTOGRAPHY BY GERRY ELLIS
ESSAYS BY KAREN KANE

Wilderness
Remembered

Photography © Gerry Ellis, 1995

Essays © Karen Kane, 1995

Illustrations © John F. McGee, 1995

NORTHWORD PRESS, Inc.
P.O. Box 1360, Minocqua, WI 54548

Cover & book design by Wayne C. Parmley
Calligraphy by Linda P. Hancock   Printed in Mexico

Library of Congress Cataloging-in-Publication Data

Ellis, Gerry.
   Wilderness remembered/photography by Gerry Ellis; text written and compiled by Karen Kane.
                                                      p. cm.
   ISBN 1-55971-466-2
   1. Natural history—United States—Pictorial works.
   2. Wilderness areas—United States—Pictorial works. I. Kane, Karen. II. Title.
   QH104.E44   1995   94-49440
   508.73'022'2—dc20   CIP

Contents

Introduction

In the course of compiling and photographing this book, writer Karen Kane and I traveled across thousands of miles of wilderness and plowed through thousands of volumes of words—words written by the long line of strangers that came and saw and recorded. Some recorded what they were told to see, some recorded what they felt, and still others scribed what they imagined in this continent still full of enough space for a mind to wander.

The explorers charged west under the allegiance of purple mountains, fruited plains and amber waves of grain, but ironically it was the unmentioned arteries of commerce and exploration—rivers—that lent early and lasting success to human endeavors.

From the beginning water lured the foreigners, possessed them and sent them to their peril. Columbus, convinced he would not fall over the edge of the earth into that place marked on maps as "here be dragons," sailed across an uncharted sea to be one of the first to reach the New World. Ponce de Leon plied the swampy reaches of Florida convinced until his death that therein lay the waters of life eternal. From the Great Lakes, the Missouri River and the mighty Columbia, men and ships were sent chasing the mythical route across the north of the continent, to discover the unseen but legendary route to the Orient, the Northwest Passage. For to the nation and the explorer who found this route would come fame and wealth everlasting.

The great St. Lawrence River was the starting point for the dream as Jacques Cartier jibed his sails around the Gaspe Peninsula and headed his two tiny ships into the wind. The seaway funneled the hopes and dreams of over a dozen explorers in the next two centuries following that blustery late spring day. And as the river opened into the Great Lakes, for each new explorer it must have seemed impossible that this was not the route to fortune and fame.

But rivers were not just the arteries of those with greatness in mind. Common folk, too, traveled still waters and wild rapids pushing farther and farther westward, sailing up coastlines and along boundary waters, and each felt compelled to record in some way all they saw and felt. Few were professional naturalists and fewer still literary scholars of the land. Often their words were roughly hewn, other times simple and straightforward, but always, they were sincere and heartfelt expressions. Each individual, however, was caught by at least a single moment when the breadth of this wilderness took them by surprise—the same surprise that even today greets those who step to the edge of the viewing platform of the Grand Canyon or see their first wild killer whale under the cry of a soaring bald eagle. Wilderness continues to inspire the human spirit, and even now, more than in earlier days, gives that spirit breathing room.

Now, as we offer you this rich glimpse of an early America, we'd like to share with you a quote by Edward Abbey that we thought of often while putting this book together:

> "I am not a naturalist; what I hope to evoke through words here is the way things feel on stormy desert afternoons, the exact shade of color in shadows on the warm rock, the brightness of October ... and a few other simple, ordinary, inexplicable things like that."

Gerry Ellis
Assateague National Seashore, Maryland

SOUTHEAST

This area that became the threshold of the new world
offered both intrigue and mystery to the first explorers and naturalists. For the
Southeast is a land of very differing perspectives and profound extremes.

Exotic islands that echo with the screech of wild parrots. Damp, misty rain forests
a thousand shades of emerald. Coral reefs and turquoise water baking in soft,
hot sun. A paradise.

Then inland swamps of palpable humidity, singing with the sounds of insects that
either bite or sting. Water moccasins moving sluggishly in brackish water, monstrous alligators that lay in wait in the primordial muck. Hostility.

A hundred miles away sweet gum trees mix with cherry and birch, hornbeam
and elm. Cool green forests climb the misty slopes of the blue-ridged mountains.
Warm summer sunlight filters through leaves to a chorus of songbirds. Black bear
and cougar and wolves move about like forest phantoms; squirrels chatter in the
treetops. A refuge, quiet and refreshing.

It goes on—barrier islands and rain forests, broad, lazy rivers and shifting dunes.

Imagine the wonder and amazement of the first explorers as they innocently
opened up the last continent to the world, stepping first into a region that would
both embrace and reject, awe and terrify over and over again. One by one, the
secrets were uncovered. Secrets, that for the most part, remain intact today.

And therefore I followed its coast eastwards for one hundred and seven leagues to the point where it ended.

And from that cape, I saw another island, distant eighteen leagues from the former, to the east, to which I at once gave the name "Espanola." And I went there and followed its northern coast, as I had in the case of Juana, to the eastward for one hundred and eighty-eight great leagues in a straight line. This island and all the others are very fertile to a limitless degree, and this island is extremely so. In it there are many harbors on the coast of the sea, beyond comparison with others which I know in Christendom, and many rivers, good and large, which is marvelous. Its lands are high, and there are in it very many sierras and very lofty mountains, beyond comparison with the island of Tenerife. All are most beautiful, of a thousand shapes, and all are accessible. Espanola is a marvel.

THE FIRST LETTER OF COLUMBUS, 1490s

Fowles also there be many, both upon land and upon sea: but concerning them on the land I am not able to name them, because my abode was there so short. But for the fowle of the fresh rivers, these two I noted to be the chiefe, where of the Flemengo is one, having all red feathers, and long red legs like a herne, a necke according to the bill, red, whereof the upper neb hangeth an inch over the nether: and egript, which is all white as the swanne, with legs like to an hearnshaw, and of bignesse accordingly, but it hath in her taile feathers of so fine a plume, that it passeth the estridge his feather.

Of the sea-fowle above all other not common in England, I noted the pellicane, which is fained to be the lovingst bird that is; which rather then her young should want, wil spare her heart bloud out of her belly; but for all this lovingnesse she is very deformed to beholde.

SIR JOHN HAWKINS, 1560s
ENGLISH NAVAL COMMANDER

Nothing is so solemn and lugubrious as a cypress grove. The darkness, the impressive silence, the profound solitude, the dangers of every step inspire the mind with religious thoughts. The depth of a cypress grove is a real poem.

ANONYMOUS

Atlantic & Eastern Forests

Rivulets of air, gentle and unexpected late in the summer, undulate across an open sea of sedge grass. A sweet perfume of drying grass and autumn rides this invisible current eastward over the colonnade of pines and transient sand dunes and then drifts out to sea.

In spring, when the eastern forests are in bloom, it is the fragrance of swamp cedar, cypress, palm, laurel, magnolia, evergreen, a variety of hardwoods, and a myriad of flowering shrubs that drifts for miles.

It has been this way for centuries—winds carrying the aroma of the inland forests over the shifting dunes and out to sea. Early explorers were mesmerized by the fragrance of these unknown forests. Though they were unable to see or explore them, they could sense their magnitude by what was carried on the wind. Many a captain's log contains a note about the sweetly scented air produced by the great forests beyond the eastern seaboard. The wilderness then was so large, so far reaching, that this phenomenon existed for centuries.

Later, when the explorers and naturalists reached the east coast and penetrated inland, the numerous rivers opened to them these wildlife-rich inland forests covering the slopes of the Appalachians. It was a bountiful new world. And it was unlike anything seen in the old world for more than a thousand years.

In summer, the forest was a continuous wave of green, soaking moisture from a warm, humid blanket of air that covered the land for months at a time. These mist-shrouded mountains, an ecological oasis, harbored a great diversity of plant life. A single valley sometimes held more than seventy species of trees.

In the midst of these roller coaster mountains shrouded in blue haze, wildlife also flourished. Eastern red squirrels chattered their agitated warning to passers-by from the boughs of evergreens, black bears raised their young among the blackberry brambles and mountain lions haunted the valleys. Throughout spring and summer, the woodlands rejoiced in the melodies of songbirds; warblers, fly-catchers, thrushes and jays.

But perhaps for those first explorers the shining moment for the eastern forests was autumn. As days began to shorten and each dawn extended frost a few miles farther south, a wash of autumnal tints—terra-cotta, cranberry, pumpkin and honey-yellow—transformed the eastern forests into a natural spectacle unlike any other on earth. Even today, the glory of this time is written into the memory of nature, and the memory of any person experiencing it, with indelible ink.

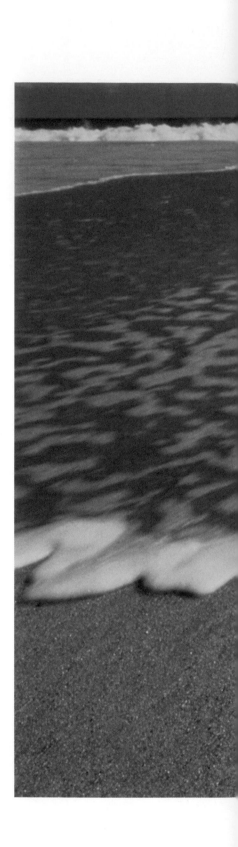

A *flocke of cranes*, the most white,
arouse by us, with such a cry as if
an Army of men had shouted together...

goodly-tall Cedars ... of excellent smell and qualitie ... about 14 severall
sorts of sweete smelling tymber trees. The highest and reddest Cedars of the
world, bettering those of the Assores, Indies or [Lebanon].

PHILIP AMIDAS AND ARTHUR BARLOW, 1584
ENGLISH NAVIGATORS

There has been, since before the American Revolution, on the island along the sea-board of Maryland and Virginia, a race of very small, compact, hardy horses, usually called beach-horses. They run wild throughout the year, and are never fed. When the snow sometimes covers the ground for a few days in winter, they dig through it in search of feed. They are very diminutive, but many of them are of perfect symmetry and extraordinary powers of action and endurance … these beach-horses … so small that a tall man might straddle him, and with his toes touch the ground on each side … could have trotted 30 miles in two hours … they had been trapped for the purpose of being marked and otherwise cruelly mutilated; and rather than submit to their pursuers, they swam of at once in the wide expanse of the ocean, preferring a watery grave, to a life of ignominious celibacy and subjugation.

J. S. SKINNER
AUTHOR

[In fall, the wild geese] afterwards proceed southward, with great cries, and hopping along with an almost incredible swiftness; at the same time there came also swans, cranes, heron, ducks and various other kinds of birds and fowls.

DELAWARE INDIANS TO EARLY SETTLERS

Before the arrival of the Europeans,

the whole country was a Wood, The Swamps full of Cripple & Brush;

and the Ground unbroke..... [The land] is varied with pleasant, swelling knobs, brooks and little lakes. In its vegitation it abounds with sweet-maples, linden, birch, elm, white pines in some places; and with goose-berry underwoods on the north side of all the ridges.

LEWIS EVANS, CIRCA 1745
GEOGRAPHER

What I saw every day and in the greatest numbers was trees. ... It is not only continual forest, but a very monotonous forest, there being little variety. ... In the eternal woods it is impossible to keep off a particularly unpleasant, anxious feeling, which is excited irrestibly by the continuing shadow and the confined outlook.

DR. J. D. SCHOEPH, LATE 1700S
SURGEON

The American forests have generally one very interesting quality, that of being entirely free from under or brushwood. This is owing to the extraordinary height, and spreading tops of the trees; which thus prevent the sun from penetrating to the ground, and nourishing inferior articles of vegetation. In consequence of the above circumstance, on can walk in them with much pleasure, and see an enemy from a considerable distance. Wolves, panthers, and tiger-cats, were at hand to devour me.

THOMAS ASHE, LATE 1800S
ENGLISH TRAVELER

If I should persuade the Painter to attempt the giving a real and strict Portrait of these Woods in Autumn, he must mix in upon his Canvass all the Colours of the Rainbow, in order to copy the various and varied dyes which the Leaves at the Fall assume; The Red, the Scarlet, the bright and the deep Yellow, the warm Brown, the White, which he must use, would give a prismatic motley Patch-work that Judgment would not bear; and yet the Woods in this embroidered Garb have in real nature an Appearance beyond Conception.

THOMAS POWNALL, 1750S
GOVERNOR OF MASSACHUSETTS

North
& Northeast

There is an identity to the landscape in the far north that is defined by color. White. Blue. Gray. The colors of the land, the water and the sky. Snow. Ocean. Ice. They are born of the same color, and reflect little else.

The animals add little color variation. Polar bears. Beluga whales. Snowy owls. Harp seals. All white. Superbly adapted to their environment, the animals of the far north live simply within the forces of nature that shape their home. The vast icescape of the far north forces simplicity.

The land also forces singleness of purpose. To those who were unfamiliar with its demands, the far north was a raging, frozen hell. Enormous seas, frigid cold, crushing pack ice, sweeping winds, frostbite and starvation were the forces to conquer. Or to simply survive.

The forests in the north also presented simplicity and singularity. Like a giant ocean, the tree cover created an endless monotony not unlike the desolation of the Arctic. In a wave of green, the forests washed across the rounded hills of the northeast, and swirled around the shores of the Great Lakes and edges of the St. Lawrence River.

Explorers complained bitterly about the dark forest, and its rocky or swampy underlayment. Both presented difficult obstacles to traverse. Mile after mile, explorers and settlers slowly hacked their way through a forest so full and so thick that the sun could hardly penetrate.

Today's explorers see a forest both different and the same. Though broken and scattered, virgin remnants do remain, their former glory still accented by clear, clean rivers, glacial streams and gentle brooks. And we can count ourselves fortunate that evergreens, hardwoods, and flowering shrubs still form a great forest that blankets the east with a sea of green as pure and intense as the shades of white in the far north.

In the first few months of its existence, the fur of the Harp Seal is white in color and woolly in texture.

At the expiration of a year the white changes to a grayish-cream. In the second year, the fur is entirely gray. In the third year, the gray is diversified with stripes of darker hues, and varying in number, semi-lunar black stripes make their appearance.

The Greenlanders designate the Harp Seal by different titles according to its years; giving it the name of Atak, or Attarak, in its first year. Atteisiak in the second, Agletok in the third, Milektok in the fourth, and Attarsoak in the fifth.

REV. J. G. WOOD, 1885
AUTHOR

Notwithstanding that the island lies fourteen leagues from shore, bears swim out to it from the mainland in order to feed on these birds; and our men found one as big as a calf and as white as a swan that sprang into the sea in front of them. And the next day, which as Whitsuntide, on continuing our voyage in the direction of the mainland, we caught sight of this bear about half-way, swimming towards land as fast as we were sailing.

JACQUES CARTIER, 1534
EXPLORER

There were other white ones larger still that keep apart from the rest in a portion of the island, and are very ugly to attack; for they bite like dogs.

JACQUES CARTIER, 1534
EXPLORER

The fog through which we had hitherto been sailing, scaled off at this moment, disclosing to our gaze one of the grandest sights that we ever beheld, for directly in front of us, rose a huge, rocky bastion, the precipitous sides of which were occupied by myriads of Awks, Guillemots, and Puffins, thousands of snowy plumaged Gannets floated in the air over the high clifts, while the water below was thickly dotted with various species. ... Among the most noticeable birds on the rock, were the Gannets, and they occupied a considerable space on the north-west side of the upper portion. Here ... the ... bulky nests which were composed of seaweed, were placed in long rows, about a foot apart, reminding one strongly of hills of corn. ... Early in the morning, when all the birds were on the nests, they presented a singular appearance, for there was fully a quarter of an acre of Gannets ... and when we reached the edge of the precipice, there were, at least, ten thousand Gannets before us, flying high over the surging waves. A sight like this ... strongly reminded one of a snow-storm, when the countless flakes whirl in wild confusion.

C. J. MAYNARD, 1881
AUTHOR

This river begins just beyond the island of Assumption, opposite to the high mountains of Honguedo, and the width across is some thirty-five or forth leagues, with a depth in the middle of 200 fathoms. The whole country on both sides of this river … is as fine a land and as level as ever one beheld. There are some mountains visible at a considerable distance from the river, and into it several tributaries flow down from these. This land is everywhere covered and overrun with timber of several sorts and also with quantities of vines. … There are a large number of big stags, does, bears and other animals. We beheld the footprints of a beast with but two legs, and followed his tracks over the sand and mud for along distance. Its paws were more than a palm in size. Furthermore there are many otters beavers, martens, foxes, wild-cats, hares, rabbits, squirrels, wonderfully large [musk] rats and other wild beasts. … You will meet with many whales, porpoises, sea-horses and Adhothuys, which is a species of fish that we had never seen or heard of before. They are as white as snow and have a head like a greyhound's. Their habitat is between the ocean and the freshwater that begins between the river Saguenay and Canada.

JACQUES CARTIER, 1535
EXPLORER

On reaching the summit we had a view of the land for more than thirty leagues round about. Toward the south there is a range of mountains, running east and west and another range to the south. Between these ranges lies the finest land it is possible to see, being arable, level and flat. And in the midst of this flat region one saw the river extending beyond the spot where we had left our longboats. At that point there is the most violent rapid it is possible to see, which we were unable to pass. And as far as the eye can reach, one sees that river, large, wide, and broad, which came from the southwest and flowed near three conical mountains, which we estimated to be some fifteen leagues away.

JACQUES CARTIER, 1535
EXPLORER

[They are] so overburthened with fat that they fly with difficulty. It frequently happens, that after shooting one on a tree, you will find him bursted by falling on the ground.

UNKNOWN, MID-1700s

... is very beautiful and attractive.
Along the bank it seemed as if the trees
had been planted there in most places
*for pleasure ... here are many cranes, as white as swans ... a forest of firs, which
are the common resort of partridges and rabbits ... a very beautiful and agreeable
country crossed by several little brooks and two small rivers which empty into
this lake; and a great many ponds and meadows, where there were an unlimited
amount of game, many vines, and beautiful woods, and a great number of chestnut
trees, of which the fruit was still in the burr.*

SAMUEL DE CHAMPLAIN, 1613
DISCOVERER

Such an infinite deal of fish that scarcely we are able to draw out our nett ... some as bigg as children of 2 years old. The coast of this lake is most delightful to the mind, the lands smooth, and woods of all sorts ... delightful to goe along the side of the watter in summer where you may pluck ducks in incredible numbers.

The further we sejourned the delightfuller the land was to us. I can say that in my lifetime I never saw a more incomparable country. The beauty of the shore of the sweet sea ... here we saw fishes ... some like the sturgeon & have a kind of slide att the end of their nose some three fingers broad in the end and 2 onley neere the nose, and some 8 thumbs long, all marbled of a blakish collor. There are birds whose bills are two and 20 thumbs long. That bird swallows a whole salmon, keeps it a long time in his bill. We saw alsoe shee goats very bigg. There is an animal somewhat leese than a cow whose meat is exceedingly good. There is no want of Staggs nor Buffs. There are so many Tourkeys that the boys throws stoanes att them for their recreation.

PIERRE RADISSON, 1660
FUR TRADER AND EXPLORER

Its peculiarity is that it is <u>all</u> beautiful. There are no points bare of beauty.

UNKNOWN, EARLY 1700s

The constant shifting of the scene, the alternation of bright and dark sides of the hills, together with the variation in the appearance of the river — one place reflecting the beautiful beams of the moon, and another enveloped in the deep shadows cast from the lofty and overhanging bluffs — altogether form a scene surpassing in beauty and effect any thing else which I have seen.

ROBERT BAIRD, EARLY 1800s
TRAVELER

The land on the southside of Lake Erie, from Preque Isle, puts on a very fine appearance; the country level, the timber tall, and of the best sort such as oak, hickerie and locust; and for game, both for plenty and variety, perhaps exceeded by no part of the world.

UNKNOWN, EARLY 1700s

Central
& Grasslands

Morning on the unending panorama that is the grasslands of
America has a soft persuasion about it that makes one feel as though they were
born here, and should never venture from the spot. Long, thin, fawn-colored
shafts of grass, mute in the lightless dawn, their tips feathered in sheathed seed
heads, dance in light breezes. Across the miles to the horizon their dance
becomes synchronized, undulating to the pulse of the morning on the soft-spoken
words of the wind. Not warm, not cool, the wind arrests by its mere gentleness.

The grassland morning wind softly delivers the meadowlark's message, the greet-
ings of a cricket, and fainter voices of residents unseen across the rolling landscape. Bison, grazing in a saddle of gently dipping golden ground, lift their
heads to flare black nostrils at its touch. The wind carries with it the breath of the
earth—flower-scented in spring, sun-baked in summer, parched in fall, frost-stiff-
ened in winter.

This prairie of grasses is earth and sky and wind and animal and bird and insect
and flower and, most importantly, the light of the sun. It is this light, in partnership
with the weather, climate and seasons, that most defines the prairie. The sun crests
in a high arch at the height of summer, awakening, then blistering the grasslands,
and ebbs low on the horizon in the dull light of winter, where the landscape is
reduced to the profile of the rolling hills. From spring through winter, the light
dances with the seasons and creates a multitude of parts that form the whole.

To those who first lived upon or crossed the prairie on foot, this rolling land
seemed an endless Eden. Hundreds of thousands of bison and large herds of elk,
deer, and even pronghorn once called the prairie home, as well as millions of
migrating waterfowl, including most of the world's sandhill cranes, and the now-
rare whooping crane.

To the north, the soft grasslands yield to an opposite extreme. Rough and caustic,
the "bad lands," as they were termed by the first explorers, offer only eroded,
dry, lifeless, and seasonally extreme expanses of ancient rock. It is a stark con-
trast of life and scale.

Banded with colors of earthly hues, the buttes and cliffs of the Badlands echo the
deposits of sediment that settled millions of years ago. It is here that the earth
reveals the forces to which it has yielded over the centuries. The Badlands are a
testament to a land sculpted by the elements—denuded and deteriorated, yielding to nature, each year revealing more and more of its inner beauty. To explore
this region, even today, one must embrace the endless expanse of what seems to
be nothingness. For in such instances, like the desert or the barren icescapes of
the north, the very austerity of the place is its beauty.

The Prairie dog is a burrowing animal, and as it is very gregarious in its habits, the spot on which it congregates is literally honeycombed with its tunnels. There is, however, a kind of order observed in the "Dog-towns," as these warrens are popularly called for the animals always leave certain roads or streets in which no burrow is made. The affairs of the community seem to be regulated by a single leader, called the Big Dog, who sits before the entrance of his burrow, and issues his orders from thence to the community. In front of every burrow a small heap of earth is raised, which is made from the excavated soil and which is generally employed as a seat for the occupant of the home....

The mode by which this animal enters the burrow is very comical. It does not creep or run into the entrance, but makes a jump in the air, turning a partial somersault, flourishing its hind legs and whisking its tail in the most ludicrous manner, and disappearing as if by magic. Scarcely has the spectator recovered from the ludicrous effect of the manœuvre, when the animal begins to poke out its head again, and if not disturbed soon recommences his gambols.

A hunter was engaged in shooting Prairie dogs, and had succeeded in killing one animal, which was seated upon the little hillock in front of its burrow. A companion, which had not hitherto dared to expose itself to the hunter's fire, immediately issued from the same burrow, and seizing the body of its friend, dragged it into the hole. The hunter was so touched with this exhibition of true, loving feeling on the part of the little creature, that he never could be induced to shoot another Prairie Dog.

REV. J. G. WOOD, 1885
AUTHOR

The American Bison has for a long period been the ruling power of the plains. Its vast herds have been the wonder of visitors.

Though yet seen in considerable numbers in some localities, there is a monstrous sacrifice of the creatures steadily going on; and some time in the near future they will be reduced to the condition of their allies in Europe.

Audubon says: "In the days of our boyhood and youth, Bison roamed over the small and beautiful prairies of Indiana and Illinois. Herds of them stalked through the woods on Kentucky and Tennessee; but they had dwindled down to a few stragglers, which resorted to the barrens, towards the year 1808, and soon after entirely disappeared. They gradually tended westward, and now for many years none are seen east of the great rivers of the West."

Though huge and apparently clumsy, the Bison is exceedingly playful and frolicsome, gambolling as we see domestic cattle do.

REV. J. G. WOOD, 1885
AUTHOR

Finding I had a few days to spare, I thought I should take a short trip to the prairie, in the beautiful June weather, and get a little sport

and a little fresh meat out of the bands of pronghorn bucks, which I was sure to encounter. ... I started out in the very earliest morning, when the intense brilliancy of the stars had just begun to pale before the first streak of dawn. By the time I left the river bottom and struck off up the valley of a winding creek, which led through the Bad Lands, the eastern sky was growing rosy; and soon the buttes and cliffs were lighted up by the level rays of the cloudless summer sun. ...

Nowhere, not even at sea, does a man feel more lonely than when riding over the far-reaching, seemingly never-ending plains; and after a man has lived a little while on or near them, their very vastness and loneliness and their melancholy monotony have a strong fascination for him. The landscape seems always the same, and after the traveler has plodded on for miles and miles he gets to feel as if the distance was indeed boundless. As far as the eye can see there is no break; either the prairie stretches out into perfectly level flats, or else there are gentle, rolling slopes, whose crests mark the divides between the drainage systems of the different creeks; and when one of these is ascended, immediately another precisely like it takes its place in the distance, and so roll succeeds roll in a succession as interminable as that of the waves of the ocean. ...

During the morning I came in sight of several small bands or pairs of antelope. Most of them saw me as soon as or before I saw them, and after watching me with intense curiosity as long as I was in sight and at a distance, made off at once as soon as I went into a hollow or appeared to be approaching too near. ... I sat up by the sage-brush thinking they would of course not come back, when to my surprise I saw them wheel round with the precision of a cavalry squadron, all in line and fronting me, the white and brown markings on their heads and throats showing like the facings on soldiers' uniforms; and then back they came charging up till again within long range, when they wheeled their line as if on a pivot and once more made off, this time for good. ... Antelope often go through a series of regular revolutions, like so many trained horsemen, wheeling, turning, halting, and running as if under command; and their coming back to again run the (as it proved very harmless) gantlet of my fire was due either to curiosity or to one of those panicky freaks which occasionally seize those ordinarily wary animals, and cause them to run into danger easily avoided by creatures commonly much more readily approached than they are.

THEODORE ROOSEVELT, 1885
U.S. PRESIDENT

While I stand listening, there comes, borne upon the south wind, a faint tinkling note that thrills me more than all other sounds.

It can not be mistaken for any other, and I know the redwings are on the way. Whatever the time of the year, there are joyful experiences in store for every rambler, but few that are more entrancing than to greet the crimson-shouldered blackbirds when they come in full force to the long-deserted meadows.

CHARLES C. ABBOTT, LATE 1800s
AUTHOR

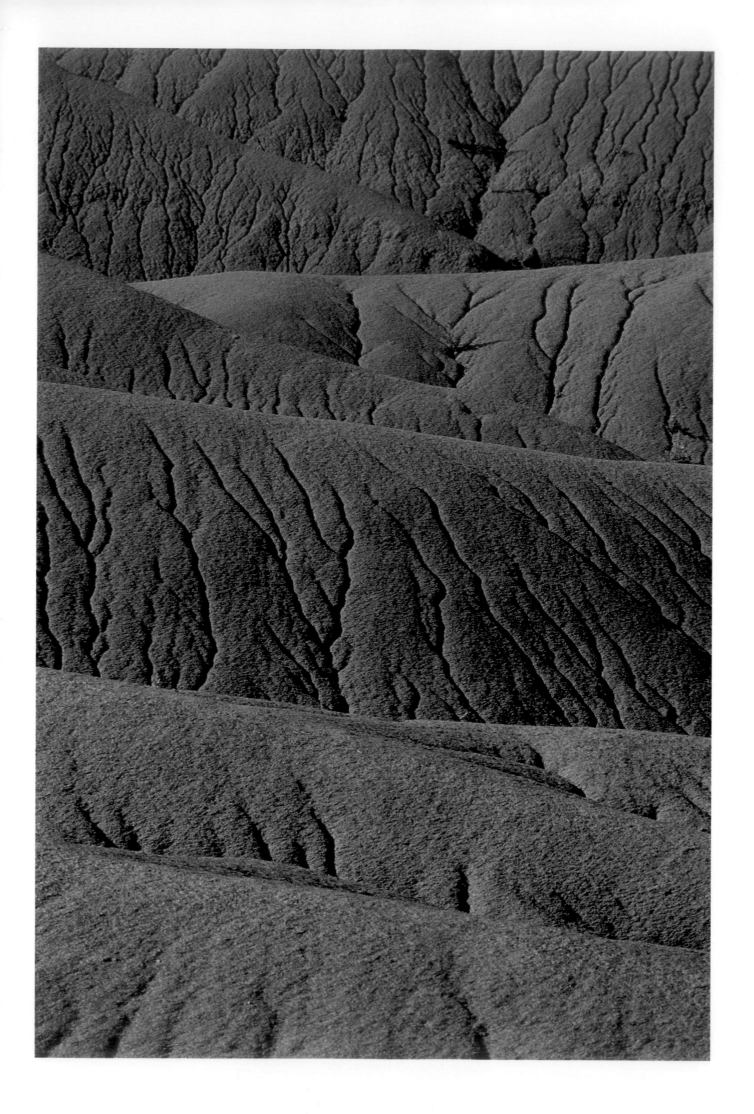

On every side arose the unique forms
of the Bad Lands, more wonderful and
fantastic than at any other point before
visited by me. Some portions look in the distance like cream-colored basaltic columns,
others an amphitheater or the shape of arcs of a circle with a vast number of seats in
many rows, one above the other; others resemble gothic temples, domes, towers, and fortresses.
The west side of White Earth creek has much the appearance of a huge French palace, and
as the early morning sun rests upon it every nook and corner seems lighted up with a
strange wild beauty. The sides of these washed hills are worn into furrows, and every few
feet there is a layer two to four feet in thickness, harder than the rest, which projects out,
forming in many instances a sort of verandah.

FERDINAND V. HAYDEN, 1866
GEOLOGIST

Many of these graves bore the appearance of being hastily made. Occasionally we passed
one marked "killed by lightening," which was not surprising to us after having witnessed one
of the most terrific thunder storms it had been our fortune to experience. This storm broke
upon us after we had retired for the night. One after another, terrific peals of thunder rend-
ing the heavens in quick succession, roaring, rolling and crashing around, above and below,
accompanied by blinding flashes of lightning, illuminating our wagons with the brightness
of noonday, while the rain came beating down upon or wagon covers in great sheets. It was
simply awful. Annie cried piteously to be "carried back home to Fazzer's house."

PHOEBE GOODELL JUDSON, 1853
PIONEER

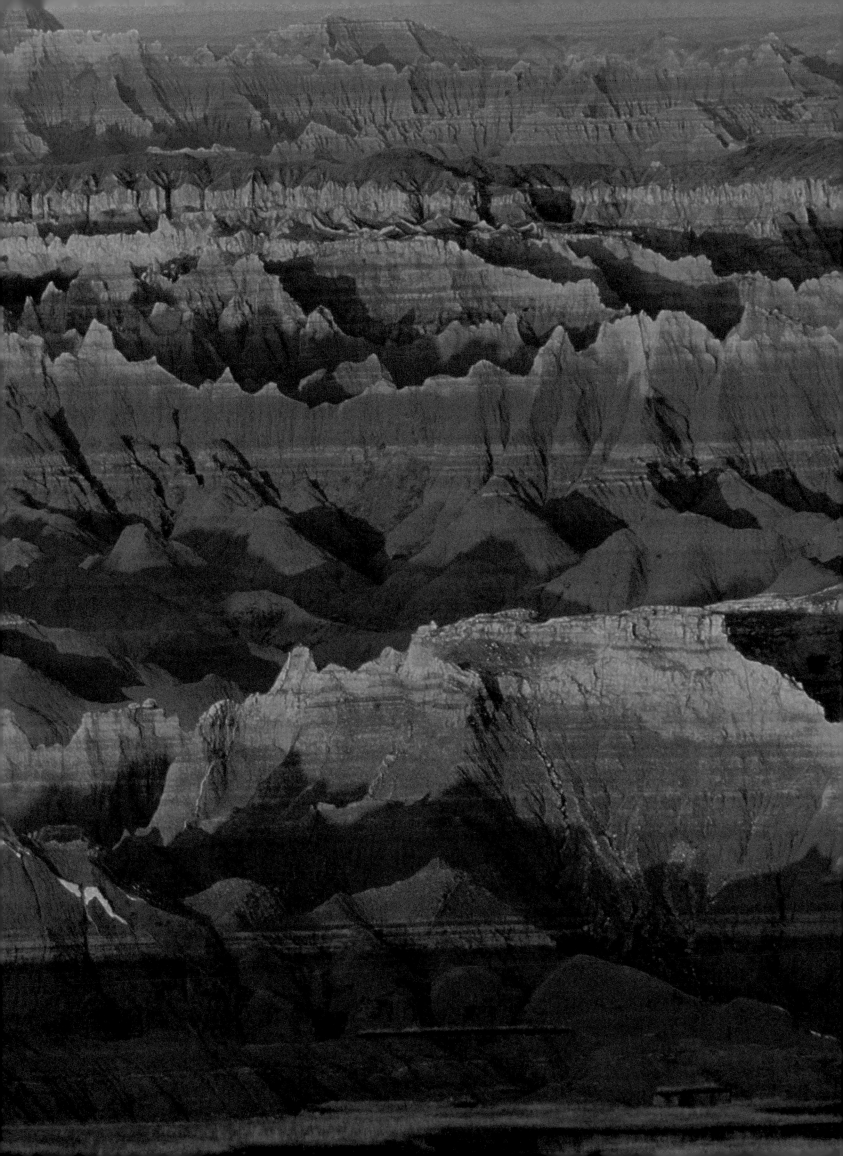

West
& Mountains

Western mountain ranges were unbelievable to expeditions sent to explore the new west. The party of Major Stephen Long was unsure "whether what we saw were mountains, or banks of cumulous clouds skirting the horizon." They were in fact mountains, the youngest manifestation along an ancient string of subterranean faults. Perhaps it was the abruptness with which they rose, a mere fifteen miles from the plains to the crest, which was difficult to fathom.

Perhaps it was the hundreds of peaks cresting above 12,000 feet. Or the awe inspiring cornucopia of geologic gargoyles—sheer walls, U-shaped glacial valleys, basalt spires and columns, thermal vents, permanent glacial ice, even protrusions of Precambrian sedimentary—forgotten tropical sea floor. Each naturalist venturing into these mountains, or through them en route to western destinations, was struck by the magnificence of the range. North America had never before presented explorers with such a challenge.

This Great Divide is the spine, unknown as it was, of an entire hemisphere. In broken spires and alpine summits it trails nearly 10,000 miles through the continent. Its presence is perhaps North America's most impressive statement of grandeur.

In what is now the plate from which the Divide was born, the earth continues to issue a statement of life. Deep within the earth two enormous blocks of superheated terra firma jostle for position, their movement creating an upwelling of magma. In this area of thin earth and molten lava, mud bubbles and boils, steam rockets hundreds of feet into the air, and springs spew forth blistering hot water.

This ceaseless subterranean activity makes this strange region one of the most unusual places on the planet. More than half of the world's geysers erupt here, some constantly, some on a short schedule, others building up pressure for more than six months at a time and bursting with the power of an awakened volcano.

The wilderness remembers a procession of pedestrians lightly stepping their way through this region, each marveling at such a wondrous place. More than 10,000 thermal features lurk under ponds, marshes, rocks, mud pits, and terraces here. This area so captivated those who first experienced its odd offerings, that nearly a century after it was first described, it was designated as the United State's first national park, Yellowstone. It was to become the cornerstone of a system to preserve the wilderness of North America, and a model for wilderness conservation worldwide.

We came suddenly upon a basin of boiling sulphur springs, exhibiting signs of activity and points of difference so wonderful as to fully absorb our curiosity. The largest of these, about twenty feet in diameter, is boiling like a cauldron, throwing water and fearful volumes of sulphurous vapor higher than our heads. Its color is a disagreeable greenish yellow. The central spring of the group, of dark leaden hue, is in the most violent agitation, its convulsive spasms frequently projecting large masses of water to the height of seven or eight feet. The spring lying to the east of this, more diabolical in appearance, filled with a hot brownish substance of the consistency of mucilage, is in constant noisy ebullition, emitting fumes of villainous odor. Its surface is covered with bubbles, which are constantly rising and bursting, and emitting sulphurous gases from various parts of its surface … as we gazed upon the infernal mixture and inhaled the pungent sickening vapors, we were impressed with the idea that this was a most perfect realization of Shakespeare's image in Macbeth. It needed but the presence of Hecate and her weird band to realize that horrible creation of poetic fancy, and I fancied the "black and midnight hags" concocting a charm around this horrible cauldron. We ventured near enough to this spring to dip the end of a pine pole into it, which, upon removal, was covered an eighth of an inch thick with lead-colored sulphury slime. … Farther along is a sulphurous cavern … out of which the steam is thrown in jets with a sound resembling the puffing of a steam-boat when laboring over a sand-bar and with as much uniformity and intonation as if emitted by a high-pressure engine. From hundreds of fissures in the adjoining mountain from base to summit, issue hot sulphur vapors, the apertures through which they escape being encased in thick incrustations of sulphur, which in many instances is perfectly pure. There are nearby a number of small sulphur springs. … Still farther on are twenty or thirty springs of boiling mud of different degrees of consistency and color. The mud in these springs is in most cases a little thinner than mortar prepared for plastering. … I can liken its appearance to nothing so much as Indian meal hasty pudding when the process of boiling is nearly completed, except that the puffing, bloated bubbles are greatly magnified. … In some of the springs the mud is of a dark brown color, in others nearly pink, and in one it was almost yellow. … While surveying these wonders, our ears were constantly saluted by dull, thundering booming sounds, resembling the reports of distant artillery. As we approached the spot whence they proceeded, the ground beneath us shook and trembled as from successive shocks of an earthquake. … the cause of the uproar was found to be a mud volcano — the greatest marvel we have yet met with.

NATHANIEL PITT LANGFORD, 1870
MOUNTAINEER & EXPLORER

This has been a "red-letter" day with me, and one which I shall not soon forget, for my mind is clogged and my memory confused by what I have to-day seen. ... I hardly know where to commence in making a clear record of what is at this moment floating past my mental vision. I cannot confine myself to a bare description of the falls of the Yellowstone alone, for these two great cataracts are but one feature in a scene composed of so many of the elements of grandeur and sublimity, that I almost despair of giving to those ... the faintest conception of it. The immense cañon or gorge of rocks through which the river descends, perhaps more than the falls, is calculated to fill the observer with feelings of mingled awe and terror. ... There is a difference of nearly three thousand feet in altitude between the surface of the river at the upper fall and the foot of the cañon. ... Rumors of falls a thousand feet in height have often reached us before we made this visit. At all points where we approached the edge of the cañon the river was descending with fearful momentum through it, and the rapids and foam from the dizzy summit of the rock overhanging the lower fall ... were so terrible to behold, that none of our company could venture the experiment in any other manner than by lying prone up in the rock, to gaze into its awful depths; depths so amazing that the sound of the rapids in their course over immense boulders, and lashing in fury the base of the rocks on which we were lying, could not be heard. The stillness is horrible, and the solemn grandeur of this scene surpasses conception. You feel the absence of sound — the oppression of absolute silence. Down, down, down, you see the river attenuated to a thread. If you could only hear that gurgling river, lashing with puny strength the massive walls that imprison it and hold it in their dismal shadow, if you could but see a living thing in the depth beneath you, if a bird would but fly past you, if the wind would move any object in that awful chasm, to break for a moment the solemn silence which reigns there, it would relieve that tension of the nerves which the scene has excited, and with a grateful heart you would thank God that he had permitted you to gaze unharmed upon this majestic display of his handiwork. But as it is, the spirit of man sympathizes with the deep gloom of the scene, an the brain reels as you gaze into this profound and solemn solitude.

NATHANIEL PITT LANGFORD, 1870
MOUNTAINEER & EXPLORER

... in the form of an immense fortification with turrets and rock-crowned battlements, and pine trees along the covered line relieved against a clear blue sky ... appeared to be guarded by large terraced watch-towers.

ANONYMOUS DRAGOON JOURNAL, 1835

The people there do not know what a canoe is; as there is no wood in all that vast extent of the country, for fuel they dry the dung of animals. There is the mountain the stone of which shines night and day, and that from that point you begin to notice a rise and fall of the tide.

CREE SLAVE, 1738
WITH FRENCH EXPLORER PIERRE GAULTIER

...remarkable white sandstone which is suffi-
ciently soft to give way readily to the impression
of water; two or three thin horizontal stratas of
white freestone, on which the rains or water make no impression, lie imbeded in these clifts of soft
stone near the upper part of them; the earth on the top of the Clifts is a dark rich loam, which
forming a graduly ascending plain extends back from 1/2 mile to a mile where the hills commence
and rise abruptly to a hight of about 300 feet more. The water in the course of time in decending
from those hills and plains on either side of the river has trickled down the soft sand clifts and
woarn it into a thousand grotesque figures, which with the help of a little immagination and an
oblique view, at a distance are made to represent eligant ranges of lofty freestone buildings, having
their parapets well stocked with statuary; collumns of various sculpture both grooved and plain, are
also seen supporting long galleries in front of those buildings; in other places on a much nearer
approach and with the help of less immagination we see the remains or ruins of eligant buildings;
some collumns standing and almost entire with their pedestals and capitals; others retaining their
pedestals but lying prostrate an broken othe[r]s in the form of vast pyramids of connic structure
bearing a serees of other pyramids on their tops becoming less as they ascend and finally terminating
in a sharp point. Nitches and alcoves of various thin stratas of various forms and sizes are seen at
different hights as we pass. The thin stratas of hard freestone intermixed with the soft sandstone
seem to have aided the water in forming this curious scenery. As we passed on it seemed as if those
seens of visionary inchantment would never have end; for here it is too that nature presents to the
view of the traveler vast ranges of walls of tolerable workmanship, so perfect indeed are those walls
that I should have thought that nature had attempted here to rival the human art of masonry had I
not recolleted that she had first began her work.

MERIWETHER LEWIS, 1805
EXPLORER

The road through this hilley Countrey is verry bad passing over hills & thro' Steep hollows, over falling timber &c. &c. continued on &

passed Some most intolerable road on the Sides of the Steep Stoney mountains, which might be avoided by keeping up the Creek which is thickly covered with under groth & falling timber. ....

Several horses Sliped and roled down Steep hills which hurt them verry much the one which Carried my desk & Small trunk Turned over & roled down a mountain for 40 yards & lodged against a tree, broke the Desk the horse escaped and appeared but little hurt Some others verry much hurt, from this point I observed a range of high mountains Covered with snow from S E. to S W with their tops bald or void of timber. ... From this mountain I could observe high ruged mountains in every direction as far as I could see. with the greatest exertion we could only make 12 miles up this mountain.

WILLIAM CLARK, 1805
EXPLORER

The pleasure I now felt in having tryumphed over the rockey Mountains and decending once more to a level and fertile country where there was every rational hope of finding a comfortable subsistence for myself and party can be more readily conceived than expressed, nor was the flattering prospect of the final success of the expedition less pleasing.

MERIWETHER LEWIS, 1805
EXPLORER

Desert Southwest

Geology . . . rocks and stuff. The American desert southwest is living geology. One can't wander through, between and under its monoliths and mesas without being absolutely overwhelmed by the living presence of rock. Walls of it. Vertical plains that seem to defy mortal imagination. And to find rock on such a scale offers still less logic, when, within feet, it plunges or ascends to an even greater extreme.

Perhaps it is just such a thing that draws, and has always drawn, the human spirit to the desert southwest. There is little fluff about the landscape. Walls of sandstone are bare, crisp in line and rich in hue. And then there is the sky.

It is the sky that embraces the eternity of change here. Sky. Wind and air. They are the dance partners in this stony world.

A crack in the sandstone, yielding to the sky, allows the wind to enter. Grain by exacting grain, the wind—now a sculptress—relieves the sediment and forms gentle, sinuous, curvaceous bends in eons-old layers of stone. Stand in the cradle of this age old sculpture and stare upward against lines that swirl and dip, twist and fall. Witness grains of sand tumbling among your shoelaces, and realize it is an evolving landscape, a sculpture in progress. It is here that the union of wind and stone manifests itself. To see the rock and feel the sky in this intimacy explains much of the overwhelming vastness that swells over one when standing below a canyon's great precipice.

The explorers who first traveled this landscape were totally entranced by this vast and beautiful, yet hostile environment. Their writings reflect the hold this rugged, yet rich land had upon them. Their willingness to leave behind any amount of comfort to walk or ride horseback through hundreds of miles of its rock, sand, sky, and wind proves that connection.

It takes patience to know such a place—and many returned again and again in search of an intimate knowledge of the land.

Since this is a hill country one expects to find springs; but not to depend on them; for when found they are often brackish and unwholesome, or maddening, slow-dribbles in a thirsty soil. Here you find the hot sink of Death Valley, or high rolling districts where the air has always a tang of frost. Here are the long heavy winds and breathless calms on the tilted mesas where dust devils dance, whirling up into a wide, pale sky. Here you have no rain when all the earth cries for it, or quick downpours called cloud-bursts for violence. A land of lost rivers, with little in it to love; yet a land that once visited must be come back to inevitably. If it were not so there would be little told of it.

MARY AUSTIN, 1903
AUTHOR

The glory of all this rock work is seen in the Pink Cliffs. ... The resemblances to strict architectural forms are often startling. The upper tier of the vast amphitheatre is one mighty colonnade. Standing obelisks, prostrate columns, shattered capitals, panels, niches, buttresses, repetitions of symmetrical forms all bring vividly before the mind suggestions of the work of giant hands, a race of genii once rearing temples of rock, but now chained up in a spell of enchantment, while their structures are falling in ruins through centuries of decay.

CLARENCE DUTTON, 1880
U.S. GEOLOGICAL SURVEYOR

There are thousands of red, white, purple and vermilion colored rocks, of all sizes, resembling sentinels on the walls of castles, monks and priests in their robes, attendants, cathedrals and congregations. There are deep caverns and rooms resembling ruins of prisons, castles, churches with their guarded walls, battlements, spires, and steeples, niches and recesses, presenting the wildest and most wonderful scene that the eye of man ever beheld, in fact it is one of the wonders of the world.

T. C. BAILEY, 1876
U.S. DEPUTY SURVEYOR

...the Country of Lost Borders.

Ute, Paiute, Mojave, and Shoshone inhabit its frontiers, and as far into the heart of it as a

man dare go. Not the law, but the land sets the limit. Desert is the name it wears upon the maps, but the Indian's is the better word. Desert is a loose term to indicate land that supports no man; whether the land can be bitted and broken to that purpose is not proven. Void of life it never is, however dry the air and villainous the soil.

This is the nature of that country. There are hills, rounded, blunt, burned, squeezed up out of chaos, chrome and vermilion painted, aspiring to the snow-line. Between the hills lie high level-looking plains full of intolerable sun glare, or narrow valleys drowned in a blue haze. ... In the broad wastes open to the wind the sand drifts in hummocks about the stubby shrubs, and between them the soil shows saline traces. The sculpture of the hills here is less wind than water work, though the quick storms do sometimes scar them past many a year's redeeming. In all the Western desert edges there are essays in miniature at the famed, terrible Grand Cañon, to which, if you keep on long enough in this country, you will come at last.

MARY AUSTIN, 1903
AUTHOR

In all the vast space beneath and around us there is very little upon which the mind can linger restfully. It is completely filled with objects of gigantic size and amazing form, and as the mind wanders over them it is hopelessly bewildered and lost. It is useless to select special points of contemplation. The instant the attention lays hold of them it is drawn to something else, and if it seeks to recur to them it cannot find them. Everything is superlative, transcending the power of the intelligence to comprehend it. There is no central point or object around which the other elements are grouped and to which they are tributary. The grandest objects are merged in a congregation of others equal grand. Hundreds of these mighty structures, miles in length, and thousands of feet in height, rear their majestic heads out of the abyss, displaying their richly-molded plinths and friezes, thrusting out their gables, wing-halls, buttresses, and pilasters, and recessed with alcoves and panels. If any one of these stupendous creations had been planted upon the plains of central Europe it would have influenced the decorative art of Japan. Yet here they are all swallowed up in the confusion of multitude. It is not alone the magnitude of the individual objects that makes this spectacle so portentous, but it is still more the extravagant profusion with which they are arrayed along the whole visible extent of the broad chasm.

CLARENCE DUTTON, 1882
U.S. GEOLOGICAL SURVEYOR

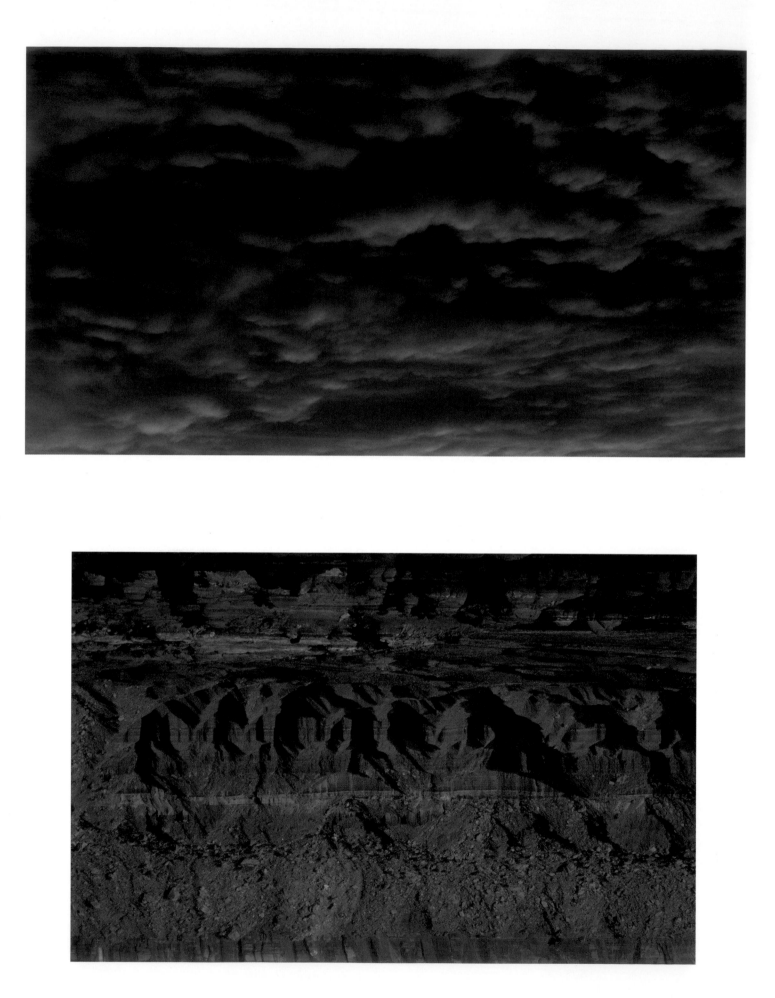

The view swept westward over a wide extent of country, in its general aspects a plain, but everywhere cut deeply by a tangled maze of cañons, and thickly set with towers, castles, and spires of most varied and striking forms; the most wonderful monuments of erosion which our eyes, already experienced in objects of this kind, had beheld.

Near the mesa we were leaving stand detached portions of it of every possible form, from broad, flat tables to slender cones crowned with pinnacles of the massive sandstone which forms the perpendicular faces of the walls of the Cañon Colorado. These castellated buttes are from one to fifteen hundred feet in height, and no language is adequate to convey a just idea of the strange and impressive scenery formed by their grand and varied outlines.

Toward the west the view reached some thirty miles, there bounded by long lines and bold angles of mesa walls similar to those behind us, while in the intervening space the surface was diversified by columns, spires, castles, and battlement towers of colossal but often beautiful proportions, closely resembling elaborate structures of art, but in effect far surpassing the most imposing monuments of human skill.

JOHN S. NEWBERRY, M.D., 1859
EXPLORER

Above the cumuli and often flung across them like bands of gauze, are the strati — clouds of the middle air region. This veil or sheet-cloud might be called a twilight cloud, giving out as it does its greatest splendor after the sun has disappeared below the verge. It then takes all colors and with singular vividness. At times it will overspread the whole west as a sheet of brilliant magenta, but more frequently it blares with scarlet, carmine, crimson, flushing up and then fading out, shifting from one color to another; and finally dying out in a beautiful ashes of roses. When these clouds and all their variations have faded into lilac and deep purples, there are still bright spots of color in the upper sky where the cirri are receiving the last rays of the sun.

JOHN C. VAN DYKE, 1901
AUTHOR

After the clouds have all shifted into purples and the western sky has sunk into night, then up from the east the moon —

the misshapen orange-hued desert moon. How large it looks! And how it warms the sky, and silvers the edges of the mountain peaks, and spreads its wide light across the sands! Up, up it rises, losing something of its orange and gaining something in symmetry. In a few hours it is high in the heavens and has a great aureole of color about it. Look at the ring for a moment and you will see all the spectrum of colors arranged in order. Pale hues they are but they are all there. Rainbows by day and rainbows by night! Radiant circles of colored light — not one but many. Arches above arches — not two or three but five solar bows in the sky at one time! What strange tales come out of the wilderness! But how much stranger, how much more weird and extraordinary the things that actually happen in this desert land.

High in the zenith rides the desert moon. What a flood of light comes from it! What pale, phosphorescent light!

JOHN C. VAN DYKE, 1901
AUTHOR

Pacific Northwest

Coastlines wild and cold. The surging surface of a frigid sea. Ancient old growth forests and alpine meadows. That is what separates North America's northwest coastal country from the remainder of the continent to the east. That and the densely forested, wet mountainsides and volcano foothills that fall to the sea.

Dampness is the one ubiquitous impression everyone is met with. For here, water is the one constant, the one ever-present factor of life to which all living and non-living forces in the Pacific coastal country must adapt itself. It is wetness that undoubtedly shaped the writing of the early explorers.

By observing the Native Americans, it became clear to them that all this water afforded a wealth of life. Seals and otter, bears and fish, waterfowl and the fruits of the forest helped to diminish the pressure of sheer survival in this wild land.

Aquatic creatures like killer whales—orcas, those giant black and white sirens—call to the spirit. After you see them once, feel their enormous power in the water around you and watch them vault from the sea with all the grace and acrobatic nature of a tern in the air or an antelope on the plains, you understand.

If water dominates the sensorial impression of the Pacific environment, then surely green overwhelms the visual. Yet it is again a vastly different world on the eastern side of these coastal mountains stretching along the Pacific Coast. Here the air is dry and dust rises. Days are hot and burning and turn with the fall of the sun to cold, crisp nights. While on the coast the ancient temperate rain forest may be in the throes of a drenching Pacific storm, the skies of the eastern high desert swell into the stratosphere with fluffy white cumulus clouds that taunt the dry earth and then push on to the summits in Idaho, Montana, and Wyoming.

One cannot help but wonder, when watching an enormous high desert storm sweeping up the Clearwater River canyon, how consuming the complexity of this new North America must have appeared in the minds of these adventurers. Knowing they tread in a way, in a place, and in a time no other had and no others would again.

... every where a thick forest of Pine, with scarcely a clear spot to be seen in the interior part; a high ridge of mountains extended themselves nearly in the direction of the coast. We observed great quantities of seals and Sea Otters; and often saw them rise from the bottom to devour large fish they brought up with them.

    ... At 3 p.m. on the 29th our friendly breeze failed us, and not being far from the shore we anchored ... the Land was every where covered with trees close down to the water side. A few fish were caught with hook and line and the jolly boat was given to me to try my luck in shooting. A few Sea gulls and a Cormorant was all I procurred. They made an escellent Pie and gave a good Supper to a Jovial Party.

THOMAS MANBY, 1792
EXPLORER

The river abounds with excellent salmon
and most other river fish, and the woods
with moose and deer, the skins of which
were brought to us in great plenty. The banks produce a ground nut, which is an
excellent substitute for bread and potatoes. We found oak, ash and walnut trees, and
clear ground, which with little labor might be made fit to raise such seed crops as are
necessary for the sustenance of inhabitants.

JOHN BOIT, 1791
NAVAL EXPLORER

All night geese, swan, and duck were flying over, to the N. W. the usual noises and infirmities broke my rest much last night.

Soon after sun-rise the clouds thickened, and occasional gleams of lightning, fresh breeze from the E. ... This afternoon another flock of the small buntings, swept by me chirping, and alighted on some low pines, to the eastward. The are of an ash color. ... Numerous vultures & eagles flying about. When a child, I was delighted to see the "Welchmen picking his geese." — Not so now.

After dark, hazy then cloudy. Cranes, geese, brandt, and ducks, flying over all night to the Northward. I slept very well, till near morning, when a indiscreet pack of wolves, near the camp, started a thundering howl, for 15 minutes.

I hear frogs croaking, and small birds warbling. — Swarms of wild fowl constantly going over to the Northward indicating that old winter is about to emigrate from here. ... The birds are scarce, and very shy, and I am weak and nervous. — The wolves will not come close enough; and if they did, my nervousness will prevent me from taking correct aim at them.

... the robins were crying & hopping about among the cedars, but flew before I could get near them. Saw a bald eagle and several vultures soaring over head. ... A flock of geese flew over to the Northward — they were low enough to shoot, but I was too weak to raise my gun in time. The blue woodpeckers are as shy as the robins. Cannot get nearer than 200 yds. of either, and have no fine shot. ... About 12 1/2 p.m. a small flock of dark cranes went over, towards the S. W. then swept around to the N.W. ... About 5 p.m. a flock of wild pigeons flew low, and very rapidly over. ... At dusk a flock of geese passed — going to the N. and flew high. Their gabbling startled me, as has happened before. Geese and cranes, when distant, sound very much like human voices. ... Night clear and mild — wild fowl flying over all night. I got on the roof of the cabin, at night, with great difficulty, and lay there some time, looking for a grizzler to come along. The night breeze moans through the dells and among the tall trees; the howl of a distant wolf is heard, and in an adjacent tree, and old owl is hooting his monotonous ditty. All else is still, here, in this lovely spot. Hush, I hear music! a sweet pathetic air, on the flute &c! — Am I dreaming? No! There! I hear a cock crow! and a child laugh! What does this mean? — Am I crazy? — certainly not.

J. GOLDSBOROUGH BRUFF, 1850
EXPLORER

... *grizzly bears and wolves every night. The distant howl of a large wolf sounds much like the hooting of an owl, and the trinkling sound* of snow-rills is scarcely heard. The forrest is still, except now and then the fall of a pine cone, sounding like a stone thrown. At dusk, the howl of approaching wolves is heard, coming up the Western dell; but the dogs take no notice of them, till they are quite near. They are accustomed to their howlings.

J. GOLDSBOROUGH BRUFF, 1850
EXPLORER

It is a singular fact, that the howling of two or three Wolves gives an impression that a score are engaged, so many, so long-drawn are the notes, and so uninterruptedly are they continued by one individual after another. A short, sharp bark is sounded, followed by several more in quick succession, the time growing faster and the pitch higher, till they run together into a long-drawn, lugubrious howl in the highest possible key. The same strain is taken up again and again by different members of the pack, while from a greater distance the deep, melancholy baying of the more wary Lobo breaks in, to add to the discord, till the very leaves of the trees seem quivering to the inharmonious sounds.

DR. ELLIOT COUES, MID-1800S
U.S. ARMY SURGEON

It is easier to feel than to realize, or in any way explain, Yosemite grandeur. The magnitudes of the rocks and trees and streams are so delicately harmonized they are mostly hidden. Sheer precipices three thousand feet high are fringed with tall trees growing close like grass on the brow of a lowland hill, and extending along the feet of these precipices a ribbon of meadow a mile wide and seven or eight long, that seems like a strip a farmer might mow in less than a day. Waterfalls, five hundred to one or two thousand feet high, are so subordinated to the mighty cliffs over which they pour that they seem like wisps of smoke, gentle as floating clouds, though their voices fill the valley and make the rocks tremble.

JOHN MUIR, 1911
NATURALIST AND AUTHOR

Far North

The far north is magic. It is like no other place. Everything is larger,
all consuming. And the insignificance of self is absolute. The north seems only preoc-
cupied with the objectives of itself. Grand things only. Grizzlies seem insignificant,
moose seem insignificant, even a thousand sandhill cranes stretching from horizon
to horizon seem insignificant. With little human perspective but your own body, the
grand landscape of the north becomes immeasurable. Lush, wet forests cover the
land. Mountains rise from the sea and stretch for hundreds, or is it thousands, of
miles. Volcanoes push their steamy heads above the surrounding glaciers that slide
imperceptibly toward some unseen destination. The tundra, with its ever-frozen

underlayment, extends beyond vision, as well as imagination. And then, there's the
ice—miles of ice reaching to the end of the earth.

Seasons sweep across the land and the land takes immediate notice. From winter to
spring, the seasons exhibit characteristics unique to the extremity of the north. Sea
ice forms, closing the avenues in which migrating beluga whales travel, but creating
miles of pack ice for the white bear to venture across in search of seals and other
things tasty and inviting. Icebergs calve off glaciers adding a special dimension to
the ocean landscape. Millions of birds make their way above the forests, marshes,
mountains, and taiga on their annual migration. The tundra thaws, and in the short
season, plants wake from their frozen depths, erupt in a sea of color across the
vastness, and retire to wait once more for the passing of the long, cold winter.

Explorers, early and late, came to the north and found themselves as much in love
with the magic as with any concrete element. The reason for this lies in openness.
Space, vastness. And an overwhelming wave of infiniteness that is equaled only
in such places as deserts and oceans.

The north transforms on a scale difficult to see. It is at first subtle, later open and
clear. In southeast Alaska, below the Arctic Circle, the land is lush, verdant and drip-
ping wet from constant rains pushing inland from the Pacific Ocean. Along the coast
and on the multitude of islands that dot its edge, the landscape protrudes from terra
firma in a stately fashion full of complex carbon wealth—trees of magnificent size
and age—temperate rain forest that originates some thousand miles to the south.
As the latitudes climb, the area's nutrient-poor soils team with the prolonged days
of cold, forcing forests to diminish and wildlife to become more scarce.

Much of Alaska and the north remains untouched. The land exists in the same form
it became after the bulk of the massive glaciers retreated thousands of years ago.
It exhibits a rawness, a ruggedness, an extreme that is not evident in much of the
lower part of North America. It is easy to stand in the wilderness of that vast landscape and wonder if you are the first human to touch the earth on that spot. There is
no need to wonder what the land looked like before native people crossed the
Bering land bridge, let alone what the first explorers saw. Stand here, now, and see
it in its virgin, pristine state, with sandhill cranes possessing the sky, their voices
echoing their ancestors' of ages past.

We were in the midst of strange scenes, hard to render in words, the miles upon miles of moraines upon either hand, gray, loosely piled, scooped, plowed, channeled, sifted, from 50 to 200 feet high; the sparkling sea water dotted with blue bergs and loose drift ice, the towering masses of almost naked rock, smoothed, carved, rounded, granite-ribbed and snow-crowned that looked down upon us from both sides of the inlet, an the cleft, toppling, staggering front of the great glacier in its terrible labor throes stretching before us from shore to shore.

We saw the world-shaping forces at work; we scrambled over plains they had built but yesterday. We saw them transport enormous rocks, and tons on tons of soil and debris from the distant mountains; we saw the remains of extensive forests they had engulfed probably within the century, an were now uncovering again; we saw their turbid rushing streams loaded newly ground rocks and soil-making material; we saw the beginnings of vegetation in the tracks of the retreating glacier; our dredges brought up the first forms of sea life along the shore; we witnessed the formation of the low mound and ridges and bowl-shaped depressions that so often diversify our landscapes — all the while with muffled thunder of the falling bergs in our ears.

JOHN BURROUGHS, 1901
NATURALIST AND AUTHOR

The chain of mountains before mentioned is broke by a plain of a few leagues in extent, beyond which the sight was unlimited, so that there is either a level Country or water behind it ... the mountains are wholly covered with snow, from the highest summits down to the sea-coast; some few places excepted, where we could perceive trees.

CAPTAIN JAMES COOK, 1778
EXPLORER

One and a half miles further brought us to
a water-shed between the Tanana and Copper,
where for the first time, was sighted the long

sought Tanana waters. ... From this, the most grateful sight it has ever been my fortune to witness
was presented. ... The views in advance and rear were both grand; the former showed the extensive
Tanana Valley with numerous lakes, and the low unbroken range of mountains between the Tanana
and Yukon Rivers. On this pass, with both white and yellow buttercups around me and snow
within a few feet, I sat proud of the grand sight which no visitor save an Atnatana or Tananatana
had ever seen. Fatigue and hunger were for the time forgotten in the great joy at finding our greatest
obstacles overcome. As many as twenty lakes were visible, some of which were north of the Tanana,
more than 20 miles away.

LIEUTENANT HENRY TUREMAN ALLEN, 1885
U.S. ARMY OFFICER

Now is the moment to witness the display of the Eagle's powers. He glides through the air like a falling star; and, like a flash of lightening comes

upon the timorous quarry, which now, in agony and despair, seeks, by various manœuvers, to elude the grasp of his cruel talons. It mounts, doubles, and willingly would plunge into the stream, were it not prevented by the Eagle, which long possessed of the knowledge that by such a stratagem the Swan might escape him, forces it to remain in the air by attempting to strike it with his talons from beneath. The hope of escape is soon given up by the Swan. It has already become much weakened, and its strength fails at the sight of the courage and swiftness of its antagonist. Its last gasp is about the escape, when the ferocious Eagle strikes with his talons the under side of its wing, and with unresisted power forces the bird to fall in a slanting direction upon the nearest shore.

It is then, reader, that you may see the cruel spirit of this dreaded enemy of the feathered race, whilst, exulting over his prey, he for the first time breathes at ease. He presses down his powerful feet, and drives his sharp claws deeper than ever into the heart of the dying Swan. He shrieks with delight, as he feels the last convulsions of his prey, which has now sunk under his unceasing efforts to render death as painfully felt as it can possibly be. The female has watched every movement of her mate; and if she did not assist him in capturing the Swan, it was not from want of will, but merely that she felt full assurance that the power and courage of her lord were quite sufficient for the deed. She now sails to the spot where he eagerly awaits her, and when she has arrived, they together turn the breast of the luckless Swan upwards, and gorge themselves ...

JOHN JAMES AUDUBON, EARLY 1800s
ORNITHOLOGIST AND PAINTER

Glorious it is to see

The caribou flocking down from the forests
and beginning
Their wandering to the north.
Timidly they watch
For the pitfalls of man.
Glorious it is to see
The great herds from the forests
Spreading out over the plains of white.
Glorious to see.
      Yayai —ya—yiya.

Glorious it is to see
Early summer's short-haired caribou
Beginning to wander.
Glorious to see them trot
To and fro
Across the promontories,
Seeking a crossing place.
      Yayai —ya—yiya.

Glorious it is
To see
The great musk oxen
Gathering in herds
The little dogs they watch for
When they gather in herds.
Glorious to see.
      Yayai —ya—yiya.

Glorious it is
To see
Young women
Gathering in little groups
and paying visits in the houses —
Then all at once the men
Do so want to be manly,
While the girls simply
Think of some little lie.
      Yayai —ya—yiya.

Glorious it is
To see
Long-haired winter caribou
Returning to the forests.
Fearfully they watch
For the little people,
While the herd follows the ebb-mark of the sea
With a storm of clattering hooves.
Glorious it is
When wandering time is come.
      Yayai —ya—yiya.

NESTIT
THE MUSK-OX PEOPLE